# Experience Art
## A Handbook for Teaching and Learning with Works of Art

# Experience Art
## A Handbook for Teaching and Learning with Works of Art

Nancy Berry

L. M. Daisy Brockman

Chelisa L. Herbrich

Anita M. Hillborn

Amy E. Lewis

Elizabeth B. Reese

**Crystal**Productions
Aspen, Colorado    Glenview, Illinois

*This handbook is dedicated to*
**Betty and Edward Marcus**
*for their enrichment of*
*arts education*
*in Texas and beyond.*

# Acknowledgments

Amon Carter Museum

Jane Gooding-Brown, Ph.D.

Mary Burke

The Dallas Museum of Art

Dr. Jack Davis

Gail Davitt

Carolyn Johnson

Cecilia Leach

The Betty and Edward Marcus Foundation

Melinda Mayer

Meadows Museum

Dr. R. William McCarter

Diane McClure

Camilla McComb

Dr. Connie Newton

North Texas Institute for Educators on the
Visual Arts

Maria Teresa Garcia-Pedroche

Allison Perkins

Kevin M. Tavin

University of North Texas

Nancy Walkup

Photographs by Nancy Walkup

# Contents

# *Experience Art* is . . .

Exciting! Entertaining! Motivating! Interesting! Humorous! Thrilling! Interconnecting! Mind boggling! Mind blowing! Mind altering! Educational strategies are no longer about standing in front of learners spilling out facts and knowledge. In fact, demands for interactive learning helped coin the term *edutainment*: techniques which facilitate the discovery of knowledge through enjoyable and innovative games. Yet between covering state standards and preparing for the next exhibition, many educators find it overwhelming to invent new games and activities or rethink successful lesson and unit plans.

*Experience Art* presents warm-up and interpretive activities arranged in meaningful ways for use with original works of art or reproductions in museums, galleries, classrooms, and homes.

## This one's for you.

# What Is *Experience Art*?

### What is *Experience Art*?

This handbook is meant to inspire and reinforce parents', docents', and school and museum educators' teaching experiences with works of art through warm-up and interpretative activities. These activities serve as a springboard for exciting educational explorations. Through their use, educators can motivate and guide learners with different learning styles and intelligences in adventurous, organized, and reflective ways in homes and classrooms with reproductions and in galleries and museums with original works of art.

### Who is *Experience Art* for?

In the traditional classroom or art room, these activities will strengthen and enhance curricular objectives and foster higher-level thinking and looking skills. In the museum, this handbook can be used by parents or teachers on a self-guided tour, by docents facilitating a gallery activity, or by museum educators designing and implementing educational programs. In each environment, learners obtain appreciation and acceptance for multiple perspectives of works of art.

### Where did *Experience Art* come from?

The activities grew out of extensive educational research and collaborations, including a handbook written in 1996 by Marcus Fellows I: Mary Burke, Carolyn Johnson, Cecilia Leach, and Diane McClure, under the guidance of Gail Davitt, manager of docent programs and teaching resources at the Dallas Museum of Art, and Nancy Berry, assistant professor at the University of North Texas. The Marcus Fellows Program is a competitive effort designed to provide a core of well-trained leaders who will work to improve the quality of visual arts education programs in both school and museum settings.

The contents of this handbook are a representation and illustration of the strength of educational collaboration among individuals with different backgrounds, learning styles, and intelligences. Spanning a two-year period, most of the activities were field-tested at the Dallas Museum of Art and the Meadows Museum at Southern Methodist University, in Dallas, Texas, as well as the Amon Carter Museum in Fort Worth, Texas. When the activities are selected to correspond to the works of art or exhibition, and adapted to suit the interests, learning styles, and intelligences of the participants, the following experiences are proven successes.

## Why is *Experience Art* different?

To create these activities, museum and classroom educators have adapted strategies and techniques from many theories and disciplines: learning styles and multiple intelligences, language arts, performing arts, and socio-cultural and historical influences. They offer educators a wealth of ways to address and connect individuals' learning styles while weaving together the different aspects of a comprehensive approach to art education, including the fascinating study and exploration of art history, aesthetics, art production, and art criticism. The applications of this approach should encompass works of art from diverse cultures and interdisciplinary connections.

## What is in *Experience Art*?
### Warm-ups

The first section of this text addresses warm-up exercises for brief encounters with works of art. Warm-ups enable learners across disciplines to focus group energy, engage their senses, and make initial connections with works of art. They prepare learners for more in-depth encounters and enriched learning experiences with art. Not least, warm-up exercises model appropriate **interactive** behavior while breaking the traditional "be quiet and listen" learner stereotype.

Since there are many purposes for warm-ups, warm-ups in this chapter are grouped by multiple intelligences. Based on the work of **Howard Gardner**, there are seven intelligences: linguistic, musical, bodily-kinesthetic, logical/ mathematical, spatial, interpersonal, and intrapersonal. See the Warm-up section for definitions.

## Interpretive Activities

These activities encourage learners to spend more time exploring an artwork or theme in depth. The interpretive activities promote higher-level thinking skills which lead to deeper, more insightful interpretations and acceptance of multiple viewpoints. On a more individual level, the activities allow informed judgments, which encourage an aesthetic encounter and a sense of ownership of the work of art and environment. These activities are successful in providing access to understanding more challenging themes and works of art, such as abstract, nonobjective, and postmodern art.

This chapter is divided into two sections: "Content Discovered" requires the facilitator to have no or minimal prior knowledge about the work of art, while "Content Given" offers activities that are more successful when approached with knowledge of the content and context of the work of art.

## Putting It All Together
The final chapter provides examples for utilizing these warm-up and interpretive activities in a variety of ways. Both traditional and alternative ideas for instruction are included to inspire use in the classroom, museum, and virtual environments. *One-Two-Three* provides combinations of warm-up and interpretive activities and examples of solutions to connect learning objectives with teaching strategies. These suggestions can be used directly or adapted to suit individual curricula. *Museum Adventure* offers parents and educators a guide to facilitating a successful museum experience. *Make a Museum* includes ideas for creating virtual museums to extend existing museum experiences or provide alternatives if a museum visit is not possible.

## Resources
The handbook would be incomplete without resources to assist educators in experiencing art. Activity worksheets and cards are ready to be copied and used by learners. The glossary section provides accessible definitions of uncommon terms and jargon; glossary words are in **bold type**. Finally, for additional information on art and art museum education techniques, a list of materials used for *Experience Art* and a list of related readings are included in the Selected Readings sections.

## Won't you join us to *Experience Art*?
The underlying premise of the contents of this handbook is to encourage creative, meaningful, and above all, enjoyable encounters with works of art: exciting, entertaining, motivating, interesting, humorous, thrilling, interconnecting, mind boggling, mind blowing, and mind altering!

Won't you join us with some kids of all ages around works of art in homes, classrooms, art rooms, or in museums, galleries, or art centers, and try these on for size?

# Welcome to Warm-Ups

Warm-ups provide an inviting first impression for bringing art and people together in engaging and interactive ways. These initial experiences with works of art increase comfort level, focus energy, and engage the senses. Following a warm-up, learners are prepared for more in-depth encounters and enriched educational experiences with works of art. In addition, learners not only gain confidence with challenging compositions, but a sense of ownership for the work of art and art museum or gallery.

Learners do not approach a work of art empty-handed: prior knowledge and experiences, coupled by strengths and learning styles, contribute to the learning adventure. **Howard Gardner**'s theory of **multiple intelligences** supports the idea that individuals learn in individual ways. To enable facilitators to develop tailored instruction for specific audiences, this section is organized by the following multiple intelligences: bodily kinesthetic, interpersonal, intrapersonal, linguistic, logical-mathematical, musical, and spatial. Diverse facilitators and learners instilled with motivation and spirit are invited to *Experience Art* with warm-up activities for a variety of learning styles.

We challenge you to identify your combination of intelligences!

### Bodily-Kinesthetic Intelligence
Cal Ripken Jr. and Jackie Joyner Kersey, two bodily-kinesthetic geniuses, possess strength in movement and physical agility. They skillfully use their bodies as a means of expression and have the ability to create or manipulate objects. Other examples of this intelligence include dancers, actors, athletes, sculptors, surgeons, mechanics, and craftspeople.

### Interpersonal Intelligence
People with interpersonal intelligence appropriately and effectively respond to and understand other people and their feelings. Without this strength, it is difficult to socialize. Talk show hosts like Oprah Winfrey as well as presidents

and teachers generally excel within this intelligence. Sales people, social directors, and travel agents also have strong interpersonal intelligence.

## Intrapersonal Intelligence

Entrepreneurs and leaders, through their strong intrapersonal intelligence, possess the cognitive ability to understand and sense one's "self." With a keen sense of who they are, these individuals are confident of their own strengths, motivations, goals, and feelings. A person with a strong intrapersonal intelligence typically has high self-esteem and self-enhancement. Often, this strength is not recognized by others unless it is conveyed in some form like a poem or a painting.

## Linguistic Intelligence

Individuals exhibiting linguistic strengths can construct and comprehend language effectively as a mode of expression and communication. Poets and writers possess the intelligence; Maya Angelou is a strong representative of this group.

## Logical-Mathematical Intelligence

Learners with logical-mathematical intelligence are skilled at thinking sequentially, using numbers effectively, problem-solving, and discerning relationships and patterns between concepts and things. They prefer multiple choice tests, equations, and tasks with multiple processes. Mathematicians and scientists like Leonardo da Vinci are logically-mathematically adept at learning and seeing the world.

## Musical Intelligence

Mozart and Barbara Streisand are two individuals gifted with musical intelligence. Musically intelligent people—singers, musicians, and composers—are sensitive to rhythm, melody, and pitch. People with this ability appreciate a variety of musical forms in addition to using music as a vehicle of expression.

## Spatial Intelligence

Spatial learners think visually. They comprehend shapes and images three-dimensionally and typically excel at sculpting and navigation. Spatial learners can interpret visually that which one may or may not see; they can devise means to represent their visual and spatial ideas, like an architect or interior designer. Artists such as Michelangelo and Georgia O'Keeffe, decorators, surveyors, inventors, and field guides possess qualities of individuals with strong spatial intelligence.

## Art Alive

**Focus:**
To develop sensory responses to visual information through role-playing.

**Description:**
- Select a work of art.
- Take time to observe it closely.
- Look for visual clues that describe what is happening in the work of art.
- Choose participants, or have them volunteer to act out the various roles of the characters and/or objects.
- Re-create the work of art.

**Tips:**
- Props, dialogue, and sounds appropriate to the work of art enhance the activity.
- Learners should look closely for details before role-playing.
- This activity is great for museum openings and open houses!
- A narrator can tell a story about the work as the "pieces" move into place.

**Extensions:**
- Interview the characters in the work of art. Decide on a newspaper headline for the story.
- Take a picture after the characters have taken their places, and compare/contrast it with the real work of art.
- Have participants write a letter to the viewer from one of the character's or the artist's perspective. What qualities of the work would they want the viewer to observe? Why?
- Try this activity with a **still life** or **landscape** and place a character in the scene.
- This activity is appropriate for **two-dimensional** and **three-dimensional** works of art.
- Connect this activity to the *Personality Profile* activity in the Interpersonal section.

## Be The Element

**Focus:**
To discover the elements of a work of art through physical movement.

**Description:**
- Choose a work of art.
- Name the **elements of art** (**line**, **value**, **shape**, **form**, **color**, **texture**) present in this work.
- Discuss how the elements affect the mood of the work of art.
- Select one element in the work.
- Personify, characterize, or act out the element with a physical movement.
- Have others guess which element is being portrayed.

**Tips:**
- Remind learners about the moods of colors and the emotions conveyed through elements.
- Encourage imaginative and innovative thinking for creative results.
- Activity can be modified for pairs or large groups, especially for timid performers.

**Extensions:**
- Consider how the work of art would change if an element was altered. Select a postcard of a work of art and change its appearance using various media (changing colors, adding visual texture).
- Choose one element of art. Create a work of art which repeats this element at least three times.
- Connect this activity to *Elementary, My Dear Artist* activity in the Content Discovered section.

## Form a Shape

### Focus:
To explore **shapes** through body movement.

### Description:
- Participants form a large circle.
- Taking turns, each person forms a **shape** using their body.
- Ask others to imitate the action.

### Tips:
- Use both **organic** and **geometric** shapes.
- There are many ways to make every shape. Can you think of another way to make a circle?
- Discuss the characteristics and moods shapes can convey to viewers. For example, triangles give a mood or feeling of stability.
- This is a good activity for groups.

### Extensions:
- As a large group, create one shape using all participants: facilitator calls out a shape; collaboratively the group creates the shape.
- Participants assume the shapes of everyday objects such as soda bottles, carrots, windows, etc. . . . .
- Connect to *Be the Element* activity in this section and to *Elementary, My Dear Artist* in the Content Discovered section.

## Gesture Guess

### Focus:
To recreate **figures** through emotional and physical movement.

### Description:
- Select a work of art with several figures.
- Role-play the figures using physical movements to convey emotion.
- Have the group guess which work of art is being conveyed.
- How would the meaning of the art change if the body language of the figures were different?

### Tips:
- Ask participants if artists consider the emotions and gestures of their figures before creating the work of art. Why or why not?
- Pair or group students if works of art include many figures.

### Extensions:
- Use **abstract** or **nonobjective** works of art to enact the emotions conveyed through the **elements of art** and **principles of design**.
- Connect to *Be the Element* activity in this section.

## Magic Treasure Chest

### Focus:
To increase perception and re-create objects using body movements and mime.

### Description:
- Group participants in front of a work of art.
- Facilitator pretends to hold, open, and explore the contents of a magical treasure chest.
- Participants select an imaginary object, present in the work of art, from the chest.
- Using expressions and body movement, lift the object from the chest while other participants guess which object is being portrayed.
- Once the object is guessed, place the object back inside, close and pass the imaginary chest to the next participant.
- Repeat until everyone has participated.

### Tips:
- Remind the group to consider various characteristics of their object. For example, if something is heavy, they need to convey this with their movements.
- Encourage sound effects and dramatic facial expressions.
- This activity is best with **still lifes** or other works of art with many identifiable objects.

### Extensions:
- Write a short description about the imaginary object. What does it look and feel like? Is it old or new? Where did it come from?
- Create a drawing of the imaginary object. If using a **reproduction**, display drawings with the image.
- Before viewing a work of art, facilitator selects a theme, such as nature. Have all participants create an imaginary object that has to do with the theme. View a selected work of art with this theme. What related objects belong in the magic treasure chest?
- With a bolder, more experienced group, have the magic treasure chest be quite large and stationary while individuals or groups go up to it like a stage.

## Making Movement From Art

### Focus:
To explore visual movement in a work of art.

### Description:
- Thoroughly explore a gallery.
- Select one work of art that conveys movement.
- Participants create a physical movement corresponding to visual movement.
- Perform movement to the entire group.

### Tips:
- Have rules for movement: 1) Don't bump, and 2) Freeze on a given signal.
- Remind participants of appropriate **gallery etiquette**.
- Invite participants to work in pairs.
- If the work of art conveys several directions or types of movement, utilize multiple participants to act out the movements.

### Extensions:
- Create a work of art **illustrating** movement.
- Create a moving, or kinesthetic, work of art such as a **mobile** or pop-up. Compare and contrast works of art which do and do not move.
- List five adjectives describing a movement within a work of art. Write poems incorporating these descriptive words and read to the group.

## Totally Texture

### Focus:
To discover **tactile** and visual qualities of a work of art.

### Description:
- Find a work of art with visual texture.
- Distribute *Texture Bags*.
- Participants feel the **textures** in the bags without looking.
- Describe the physical textures without using the object's name.
- With a selected work of art, locate visual textures that correspond to the textures in the bag.
- Describe the physical texture, what the visual texture resembles, and discuss similarities and differences.

### Tips:
- Allow the group to feel the physical texture of the object after the description. Does the physical texture match the visual texture the viewer selected or could it fit with another visual texture?
- Participants can switch bags.
- At the end, participants look in the bag. Has your impression of the texture changed?
- Vary the number of textures in the bag.

### Extensions:
- Participants create a drawing based on the physical texture inside their bag.
- Write five adjectives to describe what is in the bag and develop a statement.
- Look around the **museum**. Find other works of art that possess the physical texture of the object inside the bag.
- Connect to *Be the Element* in this section.

### Materials:
*Texture bags*: small **opaque** cloth bags with small, textured objects (feathers, rocks, grass, rope, fabric, screen, etc.) inside.

## Wake-up Body

### Focus:
To stimulate concentration through body movement.

### Description:
- Lie on the floor with eyes closed and body relaxed.
- Begin moving body parts, one at a time.
- Begin by wiggling your toes, flexing your feet, and twisting your ankles . . . etc.
- Continue until standing upright on your feet.

### Tips:
- Concentrate on each section of the body.
- Through a discussion, connect concentration of the body to the concentration of the artist while creating a work of art.
- Listen to slow, quiet music.

### Extensions:
- After "waking-up," draw or paint the particular thoughts you had while lying down and listening to the music.
- Choose upbeat music or music from another time period. How does different music change your thoughts?

*Hina*, 1990–91, Deborah Butterfield, Collection of the Modern Art Museum of Fort Worth. Purchase mmade possible by a Gift from Web Maddox Trust.

## 1-800-ART-TALK

**Focus:**
To create a descriptive conversation about a work of art.

**Description:**
- Two participants have a phone conversation about a work of art.
- Assign them the roles of a gallery owner and a customer.
- Position the customer so that the work of art cannot be seen.
- The gallery owner must persuade the customer to buy the work, sight unseen.
- The gallery owner verbally provides a detailed description of the work, so the customer can visualize an accurate mental picture.
- Prompt the customer to ask relevant and meaningful questions.
- Finally, show the customer the work of art and ask how it differs from the mental picture.

**Tips:**
- For younger groups, provide a list of questions for the customer to ask the gallery owner.
- Remind participants to use appropriate art vocabulary.

**Extensions:**
- Have pairs create an advertisement of the work as if the gallery owner were to send it electronically (e-mail or fax) to the customer.
- Have several students participate in a conference call including the artist, an art historian, the gallery owner, and the customer. How would their perspectives change the conversation of the sale? Are multiple perspectives important to consider when purchasing works of art? Consider researching information on the work for each character's point of view.
- Have learners assume the role of two friends visiting the gallery; one is visually impaired. Describe the painting so that they can see it with the other's "mind's eye."
- Connect this activity with *Art for Sale* in the Linguistic section.

## Back Track

**Focus:**
To increase attention to verbal instruction and memorization skills.

**Description:**
- Quickly give your audience a set of five instructions without any explanation. For example:
  1) Wave at Christopher.
  2) Walk over to the water fountain.
  3) Tiptoe back to the center of the circle.
  4) Touch both shoes.
  5) Wink ten times at the ceiling.
- Choose a participant to complete each task in sequence without having them repeated.
- If the first participant is not successful, select a second volunteer, and then a third, and so on.
- Repeat until the five steps are successfully accomplished.

**Tips:**
- Vary the difficulty of the directions and the focus of the activity to match age level and audience type.
- If in a museum, help students remember to observe appropriate museum etiquette when carrying out each task.
- Relate instructions appropriate to the teaching environment.

**Extensions:**
- Have different leaders call out the instructions.
- Give instructions pertinent to art techniques or works of art in the room. For example:
  1) Draw a diagonal line on the board.
  2) Walk to an Impressionist painting, etc.
- Discuss the necessity of following directions in art. For example, what would happen if the steps of an art process were altered?
- Connect this activity to *Step by Step* in the Logical-Mathematical section.

## If Art Could Talk . . .

**Focus:**
To characterize art from visual clues.

**Description:**
- Learners select a work of art.
- Ask them to imagine what it would say if the work of art possessed the ability to "talk."
- Write a "statement" the work would make verbally.
- Encourage participants to justify the statements with visual clues.

**Tips:**
- Encourage learners to include the work of art's title, date and artist.
- Challenge the audience to be creative and dramatic. Consider the "character" or "personality" of the piece.
- Model an example and discuss with the group how visual clues in the work contribute to the development of the statement.

**Extensions:**
- Pair students and have their works of art carry on a conversation. Are their images friends or not? Why or why not? Do they have anything to say about the works of art around them?
- Ask participants to create a short dialogue or skit from their statements in groups of three or four, given the following sites: (1) elegant dinner party, (2) rock concert, (3) in line at the grocery store, (4) graduation.
- Have participants prepare a campaign speech from their statements, assuming that their work of art is running for office.
- Try connecting this activity to the *Personality Profile* activity in this section.

**Materials:**
Paper, pens or pencils

## Matching Metaphors

**Focus:**
To describe imagery through creative use of language.

**Description:**
- Divide participants into two groups and assign different sections of the gallery.
- Have each group choose three works of art within their section.
- Write metaphors for each of the three works.
- After both groups write their metaphors, gather into one large group.
- Read each metaphor.
- Allow the opposite group the opportunity to guess which work of art best fits the written statement.
- Discuss results and any new perspectives resulting from their creative writing experiences.

**Tips:**
- Metaphors can be as easy as "The wind is a train coming through the valley," and as complex as "The mountains, an incoming army, march heroically across the plains."
- Younger audiences could make descriptive phrases or similes instead of metaphors.

**Extensions:**
- After the discussion, the participants can further develop the metaphors into poetry or prose and present them to the group.
- Provide the group phrases or excerpts from poetry. Have learners find connections between excerpts and metaphors, and discuss relevance. Incorporate metaphors with the phrases to create a collaboratively written piece corresponding to a work of art.
- Have each group present their metaphor dramatically, like playing charades. Allow time for the rest of the group to guess the metaphor as well as the work of art it reflects.

**Materials:**
Paper, pens or pencils

## Personality Profile

**Focus:**
To personify a portrait.

**Description:**
- Select a work of art, preferably a portrait.
- Ask participants to complete the *Personality Profile* worksheet based on the work of art.
- Present profiles and discuss.
- Support answers with visual clues.

**Tips:**
- This activity works best in a gallery with portraits or figures present in the work.
- You may choose one image to have the whole group work with, or allow them to select the work of art on their own.
- You may choose to have the audience work in pairs.
- If focusing on one image, you may want to place a black and white image at the top of the worksheet to resemble a newspaper article.
- Prompts can be adapted to suit individual needs or interests.

**Extensions:**
- Have audience write biographies or newspaper articles about their characters and read them to the group.
- Select other works of art the characters might want to have as friends.
- Connect this activity with *Being Art* in the Bodily-Kinesthetic section.

**Materials:**
*Personality Profile* worksheet (located in Chapter 4), pens or pencils

## Take a Visual Walk

**Focus:**
To strengthen observation skills and explore multiple perspectives.

**Description:**
- Lead participants on a slow walk through the galleries.
- After the walk, group the audience outside the gallery.
- Have participants share one thing which made a significant impression on them.
- Note the variety of answers produced by the participants and discuss why they observed different things.
- If the group walked through a second time, would they notice anything different?
- Although everyone walked the same path, did everyone have identical experiences with the works of art?

**Tips:**
- Allow the group to carry on a conversation while they are discovering the gallery.
- Be considerate of those at the end of the line.

**Extensions:**
- Walk through a second time. Ask participants to write five new observations and discuss why they missed these the first time. Why is it important to carefully observe our own environments? Do you think most people are as perceptive as they should be? Were they influenced by their peers? How might viewers become more perceptive?
- Inform participants of intentions before beginning this activity.
- How would this work change if the museum environment was different? What if these works were in a mall or a parking garage?

## Two of a Kind

**Focus:**

To match visual clues and justify interpretation.

**Description:**

- Distribute pictures of people's faces.
- Look carefully at the image and consider what kind of personality is conveyed by studying the visual clues.
- Ask participants to find a work of art that the people in their pictures might choose for themselves.
- Gather the group and present discoveries.
- Discuss and compare the two images.
- Discuss stereotypes and how it is not always possible to "judge a book by its cover."

**Tips:**

- Select images of popular personalities.
- Where would the personality display the chosen work?

**Extensions:**

- Before participants present their connections, have audience guess which work of art was selected. How might someone else choose a different work of art for similar reasons?
- Write a letter from the person in the photograph to a friend describing the new work of art and why it was selected.
- Reverse the sequence of this activity: Ask your group to find a work of art, looking carefully at its visual properties. Give them a selection of photographs. Have them choose the person which most appropriately suits their work of art.
- Connect this activity to *You're Invited* in the Discovering Content section.

## A Friend for Life

**Focus:**
To explore works of art by establishing personal, meaningful connections.

**Description:**
- Explore a gallery.
- Have each participant select a work of art to be a new friend.
- Why would the work of art be a good friend? Use visual clues for support.
- Participants introduce their new friends, justifying selections.
- Encourage questions like: What makes your friend special? or What does your friend like to do?

**Tips:**
- Discuss qualities of a good friend. Are these qualities related to what we look for in a work of art? Why or why not?
- Subject matter can include non-figurative works of art.

**Extensions:**
- Write a letter to the new friend. What do you want to know about your friend? What questions would you ask? Trade letters. Ask participants to assume the perspective of the selected work of art and respond to the questions.
- Consider the personality of the artist rather than the specific work. Ask the audience to find a work made by someone they would want as a new friend. Discuss why.
- Complete the activity, then give the group contextual information for each work of art. Is this still a work of art you want as a friend? Why or why not? How did the initial impressions change? How does this relate to initial responses to friends?
- Write five qualities of a good friend on separate pieces of paper. Ask the group to place each word near a painting with which it corresponds. Read each set of words and discuss how they correlate to the content of the work. Connect with *Word Search* in the Linguistic section.

## I Packed My Bag

**Focus:**
To explore a work of art through personal judgment of visual clues.

**Description:**
- Select a work of art you would like to step into or visit.
- Name five objects you would choose to take with you on your visit.
- Discuss the visual clues that support these choices.

**Tips:**
- Have physical objects available as possible props for the adventure.

**Extensions:**
- Name the five things that you would take as souvenirs from the work of art.
- Using the entire alphabet, or a single letter of the alphabet, have learners choose objects beginning with the assigned letter. Adapt this to a memory challenge game and ask each participant to recite all items in order on their turn.

## Self-Connect

**Focus:**
To create personal connections with works of art.

**Description:**
- Distribute activity cards to each participant.
- Allow time to explore a gallery.
- Look for works in response to the cards.
- Once selected, regroup and share responses.
- Compare similar answers and explore reasoning behind decisions.

**Tips:**
- Remind the audience that everyone's opinions are valid, especially when justified.
- Encourage respectful listening.
- For a quicker warm-up, use one card per participant.

**Extensions:**
- Have student lay down the cards under corresponding art, and then walk around the gallery to discuss choices. Consider which works of art were and were not chosen and discuss.
- Adapt to *Be a Curator* activity in the Content Discovered section.
- Make your own cards or connect with *Learning through Lenses* in the Content Discovered section. For a more colorful version, create interesting shapes for each question on brightly colored paper.

**Materials:**
One set of activity cards for each participant (located in Chapter 4).

## Top Five

**Focus:**
To promote higher-level thinking and inquiry skills.

**Description:**
- Participants view works of art in a gallery.
- Learners select one work of art which intrigues them.
- Participants write 5 questions that they would like to have answered about the work of art.
- Present questions and discuss.

**Tips:**
- How could you learn more about this work of art?

**Extensions:**
- Have the group think about one work of art. Write questions on a large sheet of paper. Group the questions and assign different groups to discover the answers.
- Seek information utilizing technology as a resource.

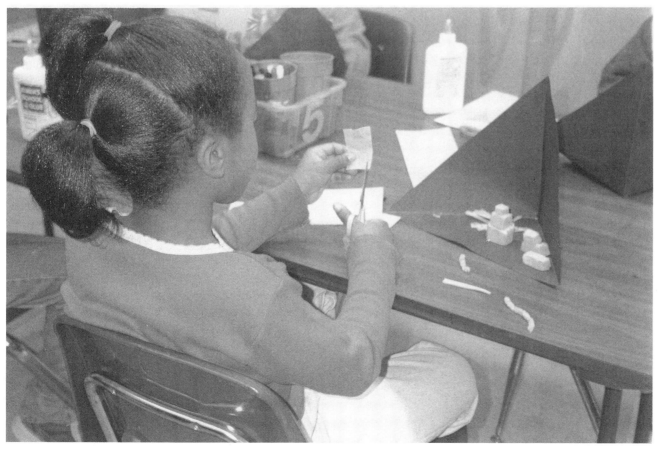

## Art for Sale

### Focus:
To explore persuasive language by creating a mock classified ad.

### Description:
- Discuss persuasive writing techniques.
- Participants write an ad promoting the sale or **exhibition** of a work of art.
- Focus on the most important attributes of the work of art to write the ad.
- During discussion, viewers must justify the work's selling points.

### Tips:
- Be sure the ad is brief and to the point.

### Extensions:
- Give the students an imaginary dollar amount they can spend for the classified, and the cost per word for the ad.
- Choose a work of art that might not be appealing to the learners and ask them to persuade someone that the work of art is of great value.

### Materials:
Paper, pens, and pencils

## Cinquain Poem

### Focus:
To enhance the use of descriptive language with specific parts of speech.

### Description:
- Look at a work of art.
- Brainstorm related words.
- Divide the brainstormed words into different parts of speech.
- Using the cinquain worksheet, select the best words to fill in the blanks.

### Tips:
- If necessary, switch tenses of words.
- Try this activity as one collaborative group.
- Use sticky notes to organize the poem.

### Extensions:
- In groups, participants can secretly choose a work of art, create the poem, and have others guess which work of art is described by reading or listening to the poem.
- With a younger audience, facilitator can record the brainstormed words and place them in the appropriate parts of speech for the cinquain poem.
- Try to create the same poem in a different language.

### Materials:
*Cinquain Poem* worksheet (located in Chapter 4), pens or pencils

## Dear . . .

**Focus:**
To explore different perspectives through creative writing.

**Description:**
- While viewing a work of art, learner selects one **figure** or object to characterize.
- Learner writes a letter or a postcard from selected perspective.
- Include the proper date, location from which it is sent, and a closure.

**Tips:**
- Make certain to include colorful descriptions of what your character experiences.
- Details might include where the characters come from, what they are going to do next, etc.
- Activity can be completed by individuals or in groups.

**Extensions:**
- After the postcard is written, participants can individually identify and draw the most important part of the work on the front of the postcard or as an illustration for the letter.
- Young learners might need an example of letter/postcard worksheets.
- Try combining this activity with the *Flashback/Flashforward* in the Logical-Mathematical section.

**Materials:**
*Postcard* or *Letter* worksheet (located in Chapter 4), pens or pencils

## Fan Poem

**Focus:**
To create a poem through **interpretation** exploration.

**Description:**
- Sit in a semi-circle around a work of art.
- First person writes a one-sentence interpretation of the work of art at the top of the page.
- Next, fold the paper (like a fan) to cover your writing so the next person's one-sentence interpretation is not influenced.
- Repeat with every member of the group.
- When the paper reaches the last person, it should resemble a closed fan.
- Facilitator opens the fan and reads aloud each statement, creating a multiple interpretation poem of the work of art.

**Tips:**
- For ease in working with smaller children, pre-fold paper.

**Extensions:**
- Audience can assume a new perspective in the work of art. For example, consider it from the point of view of a **figure** or object in the work, or something outside the perimeter of the work. Write a description from the new point of view as an alternate interpretation.
- Connect this activity with the *Cinquain Poem* and *Word Search* in the Linguistic section.

**Materials:**
Paper, pen or pencil

## Two of a Kind

### Focus:
To collaboratively explore a work of art using language.

### Description:
- While looking at a work of art, have learners brainstorm related words.
- Write words on sticky notes.
- Categorize the words into different parts of speech and physically place them in a summative sentence that best describes the work of art.

### Tips:
- If working with **reproductions**, have learners place the sticky notes directly onto the reproduction.
- In a museum, place sticky notes on the floor below the work of art.
- All the words generated in the brainstorm do not have to be used.
- This activity can be done individually or in groups.

### Extensions:
- Brainstorm the words, then have the groups switch works and words before making summative sentences.
- Select certain parts of speech, like nouns and adjectives, to brainstorm.
- Connect this activity with the *Cinquain Poem* activity in the Linguistic section or write a **haiku** poem.

### Materials:
Sticky notes, pens or pencils

## Travel Brochure

### Focus:
To create a persuasive brochure for a journey into a work of art.

### Description:
- Learners look at a work of art.
- Create a travel brochure advertising vacations at the site of the work of art.
- Focus on the work of art's most inviting aspects; think of descriptive phrases and appealing details.

### Tips:
- **Seascapes** or **landscapes** are particularly appropriate for this activity.

### Extensions:
- Use a **contemporary** work of art which contains a title of an actual place or a **nonobjective** work without a recognizable location.
- Train students as **docents** and have them give a tour of the works as exotic places to visit.
- Give information about the work of art and artist. Consider writing the brochure from the artist's point of view.
- Connect this activity with *Art for Sale* in the Linguistic section.

### Materials:
Paper, pens or pencils

## Word Search

### Focus:
To use vocabulary as a catalyst for interpretation.

### Description:
- Have the group gather around a selected work of art.
- Distribute one small slip of paper to each participant.
- Participants write one word that describes the work of art.
- Place the words below the work of art.
- Read the words aloud while participants look at the work of art.
- Discuss how students' words are alike/different.
- Which words are surprising or change the way learners view the work?

### Tips:
- Remind participants that each individual comes to a work of art with a personal set of prior knowledge and experiences.
- Encourage respect for multiple points of view.
- Try this activity again after learners are more aware of **content**.

### Extensions:
- Find connections to works of art through the words. If the gallery contains a theme, see if there are any connections with the words. **Mind map** or **web** possible connections on a large sheet of paper.
- Divide into groups and do the word search with several works of art.
- Connect this activity with the *Cinquain Poem* in the Linguistic section.

### Materials:
Paper, pens or pencils

## Flashback/Flashforward

**Focus:**
To discover how cultures change throughout time as documented by artists.

**Description:**
- Select a work of art.
- Discuss clues the artist offers viewers to identify subject, time, and place.
- If the artist re-created the work in 1950 how would it be different? 1999 **A.C.E.**? 2050 **A.C.E.**? 3000 **B.C.E.**?

**Tips:**
- Send learners into a magic time machine to investigate culture in the future or past.

**Extensions:**
- Consider how different **cultures** would create a work with a similar meaning. How do clues—**signs** and **symbols**—change within different cultures?
- Connect with *Dear . . .* in the Linguistic section and *Play Three* in the Musical section.

## JeopARTy!

**Focus:**
To promote divergent thinking, looking, and questioning strategies.

**Description:**
- Select a work of art.
- State an answer which might be derived from viewing it.
- Have audience respond with questions which could lead to the answers.
- Repeat the process in a game show format.

**Tips:**
- Model the activity before beginning. Start with an obvious answer based on observation, then move to challenging answers which may lead to interpretation and need for content or context.
- Play *JeopARTy!* with props similar to the popular TV game show and compete for "art points."

**Extensions:**
- After offering learners a more challenging answer, ask each participant or group to create questions.
- Make a **mind map** or **web** of all of the questions showing their connections. Are the questions all the same or different? Discuss how individuals not only interpret a work of art differently but how their strategies may differ as well.
- Connect to *Experience Art* in Content Discovered section.

**Materials:**
Paper, pens, pencils; cards with your answers

## Puzzling

**Focus:**
To strengthen looking skills though manipulating puzzle pieces.

**Description:**
- Select a work of art and look carefully.
- Provide puzzles made from reproductions (postcards) of the same work.
- Learners reconstruct the work of art using the puzzle pieces.
- Follow with a discussion of new discoveries of the work of art.

**Tips:**
- If the work of art is very abstract or non-objective, allow participants to view the work of art for enough time so that they have a thorough idea of its composition.
- Ensure concentration: set a time limit for constructing puzzles.
- For younger students, try cutting the puzzle into larger pieces or offering an easy, intermediate, and/or advanced version.

**Extensions:**
- Cut several postcards of the same work of art to create several totally different puzzles. Try accentuating colors, shapes, or compositional techniques utilized by the artist. After groups complete the puzzle, ask them what they think the artist emphasized while creating the work. Do the answers differ? Why or why not?
- Either before or after reconstructing the puzzle postcard, learners use the pieces to create a totally new work of art. How is their new work different from the original work of art. What similarities exist?
- Have students try to complete the puzzle without using the real work of art as a reference.
- Magnetize puzzle for use with a magnetic board as an activity center for independent exploration.
- Connect with *The Real Thing, Baby!* activity in this section.

**Materials:**
Reproductions, such as postcards or posters, cut into varying puzzle pieces.

## Step by Step

**Focus:**
To understand the importance of process in creating a work of art.

**Description:**
- Select a work of art.
- Learners guess the steps and sequence the artist used to create it.
- Provide information on the technical process.
- Look for visible clues of each step in the work of art.
- Have the group reconsider their original guess and identify correct sequence.

**Tips:**
- Learners can work in groups.
- Using shuffled cards with a step on each card, pairs can organize cards (steps) in the most logical order.

**Extensions:**
- Before studying a process or viewing a related **exhibition**, have the class work in groups to discover the process. Each group can present a stage of the process.
- Before researching the process, participants create and discuss a fantasy or imaginary step-by-step sequence of how a selected work of art could have been created. Compare these imaginary steps to the real ones. Is it possible for artists to break with the traditional steps and try new ones?
- Learners document their process, both mental and technical, in a journal and present it with the art work during critique.
- Participants re-create a piece of art in a different **medium** (i.e., a painting from a sculpture). How does the change of medium affect the meaning of the work?
- Connect with *Back Track* in Intrapersonal section.

## The Real Thing, Baby!

**Focus:**
To compare and contrast a real work of art with a **reproduction.**

**Description:**
- At the museum, distribute postcards of works of art which will be seen on the tour.
- Participants complete *The Real Thing, Baby!* worksheet while looking at the postcard.
- Take a tour.
- Participants raise hands when "their" work of art is approached.
- How is the reproduction similar or different to the real thing? Why is it important for viewers to recognize these qualities?

**Tips:**
- Pay close attention to colors, size, and surface qualities of the work of art.

**Extensions:**
- Using the same work, compare and contrast different reproductions: postcards, posters, on-line or digitized images, images in books—both black and white and color. How does the reproduction **medium** affect comparison with the real thing?
- With older or more mature groups, divide into pairs or smaller groups. Give each group a postcard. Ask them to complete provided questions in the **gallery** with the work of art. Rally groups and share findings.
- Give a detail of the postcard and magnifying glass to participants. Guess what the rest of the work of art looks like.
- Connect with *Puzzling* in this section.

**Materials:**
Postcards, *The Real Thing, Baby!* worksheet, pen or pencil

## Weather Report

**Focus:**
To determine time and environment of a work of art.

**Description:**
- Look at a work of art.
- Discuss how artists provide clues in a work of art.
- Audience writes or explains a possible weather report for a work of art based on discussed clues.

**Tips:**
- Consider the location, season, or any activity occurring in the work.

**Extensions:**
- Research the location of the work: seasonal changes, foliage, fauna (or animals), and industry. Record its annual weather report including rainfall and other possible conditions.
- How would the work of art look different if it were created in a different climate? With different foliage?
- Connect with *Travel Brochure* in Linguistics section.

**Materials:**
Paper, pen, and pencil

## Musical Drawings

**Focus:**
To link qualities of music to qualities of art through drawing experiences.

**Description:**
- Distribute sheets of blank paper and colored pencils (museum) or markers (classroom or home) to all participants.
- Play music while participants look at a work of art.
- As the music plays, the learner draws on the paper, intuitively reacting to the visual and aural (or musical) clues.
- When the music stops, learners have an **interpretive** drawing based on hearing the music and looking at a work of art.

**Tips:**
- Allow enough time on each selection of music for participants to respond adequately.
- Encourage participants to draw what they feel.
- Explain that the drawings do not have to be **representational**.

**Extensions:**
- For a large group, place a large sheet of butcher paper on a table. Have groups walk around the table drawing with the **rhythm** of the music. If the music changes, have the participants change directions.
- Instead of markers or colored pencils, have the group bring their favorite **medium**.
- When the music changes, have the learners change the medium they are using.
- Connect activity with *Word Search* in the Linguistic section.

**Materials:**
Paper, varied media, music selection, audio equipment

## Name That Tune

**Focus:**
To link qualities of music to qualities of art.

**Description:**
- Select several works of art for learners to view.
- Participants choose familiar popular songs to match with works of art.
- Learners provide support for their choices.

**Tips:**
- Promote lyrics with positive messages and subject matter.

**Extensions:**
- After students have studied a work of art intently, have them bring a sample of a song which matches the work of art.
- Participants could facilitate a **gallery** activity utilizing a work of art and selected music.
- Connect this activity with *JeopARTy* in the Logical-Mathematical section by substituting music for the answers.

**Materials:**
Audio equipment, selected music

## Play Three

**Focus:**
To link qualities of music to qualities of art.

**Description:**
- Look closely at a work of art.
- Play three different types of music.
- Discuss how perceptions of the art change with different styles of music.

**Tips:**
- Incorporate a wide range of musical styles.

**Extensions:**
- Play a selection of music. Audience guesses which works were created during the same era. Next, participants create a timeline. Compare the music and the work of art to the year when they were created.
- List similar qualities of artistic and musical selections. Create a **Venn diagram** comparing the two.
- Provide instruments for students to create three very different selections of music and have the group decide with which work it corresponds.
- Play three selections of music. Students role-play artists standing at an imaginary canvas on an easel and miming the motions of painting dramatically to the music.
- Connect this activity with *Flashback/Flashforward* in the Logical-Mathematical section and the *Compare and Contrast* in the Content Discovered section.

**Materials:**
Selections of music, audio equipment

## Sound Symphony

**Focus:**
To explore the variety of sound implied in art.

**Description:**
- Learners gather in a group as close as possible to a work of art.
- Participants look very closely.
- Identify objects and their potential sounds.
- Group brainstorms and models sounds.
- Divide participants into different sound groups.
- Like a conductor, give each group a signal when to start their part of the sound symphony, when to make the sounds even louder/quieter, and when to stop the sound symphony.

**Tips:**
- This is a good activity to start a tour or a lesson; it prepares the audience for **interactive** participation.
- Make sure everyone has a sound to create.
- Use instruments to accompany the performance. Music educators can be an excellent resource for this activity.

**Extensions:**
- Use with **nonobjective** art and have participants create noises for the different **elements** and **principles** of the work.
- Follow-up this activity with the *Art Alive* in the Bodily-Kinesthetic section.

## Apples to Apples

**Focus:**
To increase attention to detail and **multiple perspectives**.

**Description:**
- Group describes an apple (red, round, etc.).
- Show the group a real apple.
- State one observation of the apple.
- Pass the apple.
- Each participant shares a new observation as they receive the apple.
- Discuss the various descriptions.
- How is the perception of this apple different from the original description of the apple? How does this activity relate to viewing works of art?

**Tips:**
- Use an unusual apple.
- Remind the group that we should look at art the way we just looked at this apple: with close attention to detail and with the realization that there are always unique differences about all things.

**Extensions:**
- Ask participants to describe a **portrait**. Show diverse examples of portraits without faces, without **figures**, or an **abstract** work of art.
- Connect this activity with *Fan Poem* in the Linguistic section and with *Learning Through Lenses* in the Content Discovered section.

## Look Away

**Focus:**
To increase observation skills and strengthen attention to detail.

**Description:**
- Give group a specified amount of time to study a piece of art.
- Have participants turn around so they can no longer view the work of art.
- Ask a sequence of specific questions about the painting: What is in the foreground? . . . the background? . . . the middle ground? What are the main colors of this part or that part? How many figures are there and what are they wearing?
- Have the group turn back around.
- Discuss what is remembered and what was not recalled. Why?

**Tips:**
- Questions can vary from general to very specific.
- Point out the importance of looking carefully at art.

**Extensions:**
- Repeat with another work of art to demonstrate how the group's observation skills improve.
- Have participants lead the activity.

## Mirror, Mirror

**Focus:**
To sharpen visual perception.

**Description:**
- Divide group into pairs.
- Take turns mirroring each others' movements.
- How do the different expressions and poses change the way the participants feel and how others respond to them?
- How do artists use visual clues to reveal their expression or message?

**Tips:**
- Participants should start slowly and build in speed and complexity.
- Encourage attention to details such as hands, feet, expressions and direction.
- Switch roles after varying amounts of time: 30 seconds, one minute, 10 seconds.

**Extensions:**
- Have the group mirror a leader or a figure in a portrait. Coach them to pay attention to specific details.
- Attempt this with eyes closed or backs to each other and use verbal description to achieve desired effect.
- Connect this activity to *Sculpt-Your Clay* in this section and with *Gesture Guess* in the Bodily-Kinesthetic section.

## Morph Art

**Focus:**
To increase awareness of form through mime.

**Description:**
- Facilitator begins with an imaginary ball of clay or stretchy substance.
- Manipulate the substance for a few seconds and shape it into a new form.
- Pass the imaginary object to the next person, who shapes it into a different form.
- Repeat until everyone has sculpted the imaginary clay.
- Close with a discussion of form and its importance in art.

**Tips:**
- As the imaginary substance moves around the circle, encourage everyone to make something unique and original: a hat, a jump rope, a basketball.

**Extensions:**
- Pretend to take a shape or form out of a work of art. Remember to replace when you are finished.
- Learners re-create shapes or forms from the works of art around them.
- Play music to change the results and relate the music to the work of art. What would be the effect of circus music? For additional connections to music, see the Musical section.
- Connect this activity to *Be the Element* and *Form a Shape* in the Bodily-Kinesthetic section.

## Points of View

### Focus:
To increase observation skills and awareness of different perspectives.

### Description:
- Give group a specified amount of time to study a work of art.
- Participants "become" a different object in the work.
- Share new point of view.

### Tips:
- Model by selecting an obscure object, like the ground, and include elaborate details.
- Include details of what point of view they are taking, where they are, how they got there, what they think is going on, etc.
- Points of view could include perspectives from outside of the work: bird's-eye, worm's-eye, from space, etc.

### Extensions:
- ▲ Discuss points of view and the control artists have in how they choose to depict their ideas.
- ▲ Learners re-draw the work of art from their new perspective and compare the changes.
- ▲ Connect this activity to *Dear . . .* in the Linguistic section.

## Scavenger Hunt

### Focus:
To find connections between works of art and the environment.

### Description:
- Divide the participants into groups.
- Distribute common, everyday objects to each group: flowers, apple, zipper, credit card, photograph, fabric, etc.
- Without explaining the **exhibition**, groups explore the **galleries** looking for works of art which relate to their object.
- Regroup and share connections.

### Tips:
- Depending on the choice of objects and the subject matter of the art, this activity can range in difficulty.
- This activity enables participants to quickly view many works of art.

### Extensions:
- ▲ Instead of using objects, give groups keywords or phrases to look for in connection with works of art. Use example cards such as: food, love, fear, anger, sunny, school, time.
- ▲ Connect this activity with *Self-Connect* in the Intrapersonal section.

### Materials:
Everyday objects which relate to selected works of art.

## Sculpt-Your Clay

**Focus:**
To enhance awareness of body language and detail.

**Description:**
- In pairs, learners role-play the sculptor and the clay.
- Sculptors manipulate the clay into the desired pose.

**Tips:**
- If the group is shy, stipulate that sculptors use language to arrange their form.
- Include the details: position of feet, facial expressions.

**Extensions:**
- Sculptors attempt to imitate a pose in an artwork that the group is studying.
- Assign each team an emotion or message to convey in their pose, such as innocence or anger. Sculptors review the clay works before switching.
- Clay sculpture can come alive. What would it say to the group, or to the artist? This game can be connected to the *Being Art* activity in the Bodily-Kinesthetic section.

## Three Changes

**Focus:**
To sharpen visual perception.

**Description:**
- Facilitator or volunteer takes a pose.
- Group turns around or closes eyes.
- Facilitator or volunteer makes three changes in their pose.
- Group looks and guesses what was changed.

**Tips:**
- Changes can range in difficulty from obvious to subtle; removing a shoe or hat is obvious, while removing a ring is subtle.

**Extensions:**
- Divide into pairs and take turns.
- Adapt this activity to *Sculpt-Your Clay* in this section by having a sculptor make the three changes with the clay.
- Follow *Three Changes* with *Look Away* in this section.
- Connect this activity with *The Real Thing, Baby!* in the Logical-Mathematical section and with *Art Diary* in the Content Discovered section.

# Introducing Interpretation

Interpretive activities offer innovative opportunities for thorough investigations of works of art. These experiences enable learners to construct and justify their opinions through a process of critical thinking. Coupled with appropriate warm-ups and the addition of content and context, interpretative activities invite learners to explore confidently the meaning of a work of art. Interpretive activities not only lead to more informed judgments, but promote new perspectives and multiple interpretations.

For the convenience of educators and parents, this chapter is divided into two sections. The first, Content Discovered, provides engaging possibilities for learners to derive meanings from visual clues and develop personal interpretations without the necessity of specific knowledge about a work of art. The second section, Content Given, provides in-depth activities based on contextual information. While it is appropriate to have discussions based solely on prior knowledge and personal experiences, judgments based on available content and contextual information provide more informed and valid interpretations.

We invite you to look and learn, to explore and discover, to research and investigate, but most importantly, to *Experience Art!*

## Art Diary

**Focus:**
To discover art through observation.

**Description:**
- Select a work of art.
- Create a sketch of it in your journal.
- Add to your journal all the words from the *Art Diary* worksheet that describe the work of art.
- Answer the questions in your journal as completely as possible.
- Discuss discoveries with the group.

**Tips:**
- Continue journal assignments throughout an assigned period of time.
- Support creative individual thinkers.

**Extensions:**
- Change the list of descriptive words to match a current focus.
- Have participants brainstorm lists of words and questions which they feel are pertinent to understanding and interpreting works of art.
- Connect this activity to *Dear . . .* in the Linguistic section.

**Materials:**
*Art Diary* worksheet from Chapter 4, visual journals or sketchbooks.

## Be a Curator

**Focus:**
To organize or select works of art based on a subject, theme, or issue.

**Description:**
- Assign participants a new job: **curator**!
- Participants select a subject or theme in art (i.e., portraits or the environment, respectively) or a current issue (i.e., politics or conservatism).
- Select works of art which correlate to the subject, theme, or issue.
- Share **exhibition** ideas, including grouping or theme, setting, labels, related educational programs, etc.
- Why were those works of art selected? Would the works of art fit any other categories? Why or why not?
- Is it important to know **content** and **context** of a work of art before grouping with others?

**Tips:**
- Ensure participants understand the curatorial profession.
- Encourage respectful listening.
- Limit the number of works of art.

**Extensions:**
- Incorporate technology and create virtual exhibitions.
- Participants to research and read provided information. Does additional information affect decisions? Why or why not?
- Select a work of art. Ask participants to determine the theme or issue within the work. **Curate** an exhibition based on the work of art.
- How do different exhibitions affect a viewer's interpretation of the same work of art? Should curators consider viewer's interpretations?
- Use *Lens* cards provided in Chapter 4 as themes.
- After exhibitions are curated, connect *Be a Museum Educator* activity in Content Given and develop interactive tours.

## Compare and Contrast

**Focus:**
To compare and contrast two works of art using a visual diagram.

**Description:**
- Select two works of art.
- Using the **Venn diagram** worksheet, analyze the two works of art by placing similarities in the central portion of the two circles.
- Share discoveries.

**Tips:**
- Several groups can explore the same works of art.
- Place titles of the works of art on the appropriate sides of the worksheet.

**Extensions:**
- Use Venn diagrams to discuss issues in art.
- Create a **3-D** Venn diagram using overlapping hula hoops and sticky notes.

**Materials:**
*Venn Diagram* worksheet in Chapter 4, pens, and pencils.

## Discover Art

**Focus:**
To explore several works of art created by one artist.

**Description:**
- Choose an artist with several works of art in an **exhibition**.
- Look at one of the works by this artist.
- Discuss visual clues in the work of art that might be characteristic of the artist's style. Considering **visual** clues, participants search for other works created by the same artist.
- Regroup and share selections.
- Do all the works demonstrate similar characteristics?

**Tips:**
- Introduce the activity as a mystery to be solved.
- Encourage participants to describe the size, subject matter, color scheme, **style**, and **media** of work of art. Use these as a guideline in their search.

**Extensions:**
- Create a timeline using works of art by one artist. How does his or her artwork change over time? Do you prefer the artist's early or late work? Why?
- Look at examples of the artist's work. What kinds of media does the artist use? Does the artist use the same medium or different kinds? Try creating several works of art, using the same subject but varying the materials used to create the works.
- Connect to the *Word Search* activity in the Linguistic section.

**Materials:**
Paper, pens or pencils.

## Elementary, My Dear Artist

**Focus:**
To explore artists' choices made through formal elements.

**Description:**
- Select a single, significant element of art from works in a **gallery**, or from several **reproductions**.
- Divide audience into small groups.
- Assign each group a preselected **element**. (Example: a square in a Mondrian.)
- Have participants complete the *Elementary, My Dear Artist* worksheet.
- Conclude with presentations from each group and discuss each element's function and role in the works of art.

**Tips:**
- This activity works best with abstract or non-objective works, although it could be adapted to other **styles**.

- For younger or less experienced audiences, consider reviewing the elements as an introduction. Use precut shapes, color samples, or drawn lines to represent the elements.

**Extensions:**
- After exploring the questions in the worksheet, have each group create a dramatic **interpretation** by **personifying** their specific element.
- Participants create a work of art based on their element. Change and manipulate the element so that it conveys a new feeling or emotion.
- Have participants write about their new perspective as the element. What do they see? Smell? Hear?, etc.
- Connect this activity to *Be the Element,* and *Form a Shape* in the Bodily-Kinesthetic section.

## Experience Art

**Focus:**
To relate a work of art to a personal experience or memory.

**Description:**
- Participants select an *Experience Art* card from a stack or container.
- Read selected statement.
- Walk through galleries and select a work of art which best relates to the statement on the card.
- Take turns sharing responses with the rest of the group.
- How does previous knowledge and experience affect individual interpretations? Why are personal interpretations valid?

**Tips:**
- Encourage students to share their experiences, but be aware of emotional responses.
- Validate all responses.
- Good activity to use with groups who are familiar with one another.

**Extensions:**
- Have individuals write responses to the *Experience Art* cards.
- Develop a work of art which is derived from their response to the statement.
- Connect this to the *Self-Connect* activity in the Intrapersonal section.

**Materials:**
*Experience Art* cards in Chapter 4 and a container such as a basket or box.

Adapted from Ray Williams, Ackland Art Museum

## Is a Rose a Rose?

**Focus:**
To **interpret** a work of art utilizing its visual clues.

**Description:**
- Divide participants into groups.
- Have each group look at an unfamiliar work of art.
- Assign a title to the work of art based on visual clues.
- Have groups share and discuss why the titles were chosen.
- What meanings are derived?
- Present the given title to the groups.
- Discuss the participants' titles versus given titles.
- Is the artist successful at conveying meaning by the title? Does the meaning change when the artist's title is known?

**Tips:**
- This is an exciting activity to do with **abstract** works of art.

**Extensions:**
- Give **content** of the work of art and see if the learners' title changes.
- Discuss the positive and negative aspects of first impressions.
- Discuss how works of art are sometimes titled by someone other than the artist. Is that okay? Why or why not?
- Discuss how some artists call their work "untitled." Why do you think an artist would select such a title?
- Place participants' titles and given titles together on the floor. Group guesses to which work they belong.
- Connect this activity with the *Top Five* in the Intrapersonal section.

## Learning Through Lenses

**Focus:**
To investigate a work of art through utilizing a new point of view.

**Description:**
- Select a work of art.
- Distribute *Lens* cards.
- Participants **interpret** the work of art based on assigned *Lens* card.
- Share findings.
- Did the assigned lens encourage learners to investigate the works of art in a new way? How did the lens change their perspectives? Is it important to consider different perspectives? Why or why not?

**Tips:**
- Investigate lenses in pairs or groups.
- Encourage respectful listening.
- Remind learners that the lenses may be different than their personal points of view.
- Write more specific questions on the back of the *Lens* cards.

- Discuss how this activity applies to other aspects of life?

**Extensions:**
- Learners create works of art based on their interpretations within their lenses.
- Use different lenses as a catalyst for a news broadcast of the same "scene." How might reporters' individual perspectives or slants affect journalism?
- Provide additional information on the work. Do participants' interpretations change with knowledge of **content**? Is content important to interpreting a work of art? Why or why not?
- **Mind map** the different groups' interpretations. How do they relate?
- Connect with the *Be a Curator* activity in this section and/or *Apples to Apples* in the Spatial section.

**Materials:**
*"Learning Through Lenses" Lens* cards in Chapter 4.

## Looking Together

### Focus:
To collaboratively **interpret** a work of art through writing.

### Description:
- Divide audience into small groups.
- Groups select a work of art.
- Each group member writes a statement or sentence about the work.
- Within the group, read each statement aloud. Collaboratively, arrange and edit the statements into a logical sequence to form a narrative, poem, song, rap, or dance. Share interpretations.

### Tips:
- Make sure interpretations are justified with **visual** clues.

### Extensions:
- After presenting group interpretations, find other interpretations of the same work of art. For example, select an artist's statement or an **art critic's** review. How is the group's interpretation similar or different from these statements? Create another narrative, poem, etc., which also includes the artist's point of view.
- Connect to *Word Search* or *Cinquain Poem* activities in the Linguistic section or *Learning Through Lenses* activity in this section.

### Materials:
Paper, pens or pencils.

## Subject Sleuth

### Focus:
To get acquainted with several works of art with a common subject.

### Description:
- Select several works of art with a common subject such as portraits, Spanish Masters, still life, farms, etc.
- Have learners follow written or verbal clues in the "gallery" of works to locate the work of art that fits the clue. Example clues are: This woman is resting in a dark room. A little boy is hugging something ferocious but does not seem afraid. This woman seems to be staring in your direction no matter where you stand. She also seems to be thinking deeply about something—Can you find her?
- Discuss the visual clues that helped them identify the work of art from the hints given.

### Tips:
- This activity is a great way to introduce a style or subject and to obtain familiarity with various works of art.

### Extensions:
- In a gallery, have the learner find one specific work of art by using location clues to find it. For example: You will find this work of art by passing an angry soldier on your left, who will be looking at a woman in a pink dress. Visit the woman and look where she is pointing. Visit the work of art being pointed out and place your back toward the work of art. Walk 10 paces and take a right, etc.
- Connect this activity to *Object Treasure Hunt* warm-up in the Spatial section.

### Materials:
Written clues for the gallery.

## Tell Me a Story

**Focus:**
To **interpret** a work of art through narration.

**Description:**
- Select a work of art.
- Brainstorm the beginning, middle, and/or end of a story relating to the work of art.
- Write, tell, or act out the story.
- Perform story literally or dramatically.

**Tips:**
- Learners use **visual** clues from the work of art to motivate and support the different components of the story.
- In an exhibition, participants view one work of art. Divide learners into groups to construct the beginning, middle, and end of the story.
- Research selected work of art. Are there any connections to the participants' narratives?

**Extensions:**
- Learners dramatize their narratives to the group.
- Several groups can write their own version of the story of what they think happened and share with others the **multiple interpretations**. Are there any similarities? Why?
- Alter the sequence of events and provide an opportunity for others to correct the order of events.
- Connect this activity with *Word Search, Fan Poem,* and/or *Cinquain Poem* in the Linguistic section.

## Visual Clues

**Focus:**
To gain an understanding of the role of **visual** clues in **portraits**.

**Description:**
- Display a variety of props that could give a figure character.
- Select two participants: one to be a sitter and one to be an artist.
- The sitter and artist choose two or three props and collaborate about the pose and facial expressions.
- Discuss how visual clues or attributes convey information about works of art. What messages are the sitter and artist conveying?
- Make any changes necessary to convey the appropriate message.
- Have the artist use an instant print camera to take the portrait.
  Repeat with new volunteers.
  Discuss findings with group.

**Tips:**
- Encourage the use of close-ups and unusual compositions.
- Discuss how stereotypes affect our judgment of visual clues.
- Consider combinations associated with professions: chef's hat, apron, and wooden spoon, or white lab coat and stethoscope.

**Extensions:**
- Instead of an instant print camera, have the artist and others sketch the sitter, or use a digital camera and computer.
- Connect this activity to *Gesture Guessing* in the Bodily-Kinesthetic, *Two of Kind* in the Interpersonal section, and *You're Invited* in the Content Given section.

**Materials:**
Bag or box of interesting props, instant print camera and film, or other art media

Adapted from Ray Williams, Ackland Art Museum

## Back In Time

**Focus:**
To sequence works of art by predicting their time in history.

**Description:**
- Select several works of art.
- Have learners place works of art in chronological order using only **visual** clues.
- Do not disclose the dates.
- Discuss reasoning of selected order.
- Give the participants content and context, including dates.
- Create an historical contextual timeline and reinforce with great moments of history.
- Compare and contrast participants' sequence versus chronological sequence. What are the similarities and differences?

**Tips:**
- In a classroom, use postcards or large **reproductions**.
- In a **museum**, distribute numbered sheets of paper to place in front of the work of art.
- Activity is successful in collaborative groups or on an individual basis.

**Extensions:**
- Combine paintings, sculpture, decorative arts, etc. with the activity.
- Learners create a personal timeline that relates to famous works of art that were completed during special moments of their lives: ex., Georgia O'Keeffe painted *Black Iris* when the person was married.
- Select one time period and have each participant create a timeline of different aspects of that particular time. For example: In the 1950's, explore technology, art, sports, music, science, literature, math, the performing arts, celebrities, etc.

## Be a Museum Educator

**Focus:**
To create a **gallery** tour based on a group of artworks.

**Description:**
- Have facilitator select 5-7 works of art.
- Distribute and read *Create a Tour* worksheet. View and discuss how works of art might be grouped and explained according to a **theme** or **subject**.
- Develop a tour utilizing the worksheet.
- Give others a tour.

**Tips:**
- Allow participants to work in groups of three or four.
- Encourage participants to understand a **docent's** job.
- Encourage learners to select activities from this handbook.

- Brainstorm other themes or subjects for same tour. How does the theme or subject affect the presentation?

**Extensions:**
- Research the works selected for the tour. How does additional information affect the presentations?
- Make a list of the commonalities between the works of art selected for their tour. How many things do these works have in common other than the overall theme? Why do you think these works have these things in common?
- Use *What Does It Mean To You?* worksheet in the Content Given section for ideas about how to develop a tour.
- Connect to *Flashback/Flashforward* activity in the Logical-Mathematical section.

**Materials:**
*Create a Tour* worksheet in Chapter 4, pens or pencils.

## Meaning-TV

### Focus:
To make meaning of a work of art utilizing music and performance.

### Description:
- Select several works of art.
- Encourage learners to gather information about the works of art.
- Ask learners to select music which provides an **interpretation** of the work of art.
- In pairs or small groups, create a performance incorporating the music to interpret the work of art.
- How do music and performance affect others' interpretation of the works of art?

### Tips:
- Encourage participants to select music with positive lyrics.
- Encourage respectful audience etiquette.

### Extensions:
- Collaborate with music and drama educators to create a large performance or video.
- Assign groups the same work of art. Provide only half the group additional information. How are the music selections and performance qualities similar or different? Is it important to review additional information before interpreting a work of art? Why or why not?
- Connect with *Learning Through Lenses* activity in the Content Discovered section.

## Quality Quotes

### Focus:
To explore the **multiple interpretations** of a single work of art.

### Description:
- Select a work of art.
- Participants write a descriptive statement about the work of art.
- Distribute the *Quality Quotes* sheet that you created.
- Participants read the quotes. Do any correspond to their statement?
- Share descriptive statements. Discuss similarities and differences between the groups' personal statements and the *Quality Quotes*.
- Which quote is by the artist? Is it important to know who said what? Why or why not?

### Tips:
- What do participants believe the work means? What do they think the artist was thinking? What might a journalist write about it?

### Extensions:
- After completing the activity, participants write a new personal statement. How does new information affect their opinions? Is it better to interpret a work of art with or without information? Why or why not?
- In a **gallery** with many different works, distribute one *Quality Quote* (all about the same art or artist) to each participant. Participants guess which work of art or artist their quote is about and discuss. Do not reveal which work of art or artist the quotes are about.
- Connect to *Quoting Art* in the Content Given section.

### Materials:
Create a *Quality Quotes* worksheet by researching and collecting statements about the selected work of art by the **artist, art historians, art critics, aestheticians**, and art viewers.

## Quoting Art

### Focus:
To construct and justify opinions about artists and art through a process of critical thinking.

### Description:
- Read *Quoting Art* worksheet aloud to the group.
- Ask learners if they share the same opinion as the authors of the statements? Why? Justify answers.
- Do you have a different opinion from the authors of these quotes? Why? Justify answers.
- Have each participant select a quote they feel strongly about.
- Locate a work of art which correlates to the statement.
- Share discoveries with the whole group.

### Tips:
- Consider placing each quote on a separate card and asking participants to read them aloud.

### Extensions:
- Ask participants to develop their own personal statements about art. Find corresponding works of art. Discuss why.
- Look at a work of art first, then ask students to write a brief statement about it. Read the statements aloud. Connect the works of art to the statements.
- Research the profession of "art critic." What is the art critic's position in the art world? Are art critics vital to our understanding of art? Why or why not? Are they always right? Why or why not? Who listens to the art critics? Why?
- Research other viewpoints and perspectives other than artists'. Consider collectors such as **J. Paul Getty** and **Albert C. Barnes** or critics like **Clement Greenberg** and **Robert Hughes**.

### Materials:
*Quoting Art* worksheet in Chapter 4, pens or pencils

## What Does it Mean to You?

### Focus:
To encourage personal connections with works of art.

### Description:
- Select a work of art that creates curiosity.
- Spend time looking carefully.
- Select five viewing strategies from the *What Does it Mean to You?* worksheet that you would want to explore.
- Rank the strategies selected, one through five.
- Discuss discoveries and ways of using these strategies.

### Tips:
- Allow ample time for audience to consider their choices.

### Extensions:
- Group participants with works of art. Complete the worksheet individually first, and then try finding consensus in the group through discussion and persuasion. Present finding to other groups.
- Create a short tour using five chosen strategies.
- Connect this activity with *Be a Museum Educator* in Content Given section.

### Materials:
*What Does It Mean To You?* worksheet in Chapter 4, pens or pencils

## You're Invited!

### Focus:
To seek commonalities through an exploration of visual clues.

### Description:
- Select several works of art. Subject matter can range from **portraits** to **landscapes**.
- Select a party theme and incorporate elements from the works of art into the party: pajama party, tea party, skating party, costume party, picnic, a party that a famous celebrity would be invited to attend, etc.
- Learners decide from selected works of art who will be invited to the party based on **visual** clues such as what the person is wearing, holding, their background, their age, etc. Landscapes provide options for locations and environment while **still lifes** can provide food and containers for the party.
- Discuss content of the portraits chosen.
- Compare/contrast the portraits that were invited to the party to the **content** given by the facilitator. Would the portraits that were chosen have realistically attended the party that was planned? Why or why not? How did participants' perceptions change?
- Discuss the positive and negative aspects about judging a person by what they look like or wear. Has anyone experienced someone misinterpreting who they really were on the basis of what they were wearing or where they were?

### Tips:
- Party planners choose what type of food, music, and refreshments that will be served at their imaginary party.
- Describe an outlandish event that happened at the party.
- Invite a celebrity to the party.

### Extensions:
- Give content of works first and then create a party. Justify all decisions of the party by content clues.
- Write a gossip column describing the highlights of the party.

*Sculpture for Derry Walls*, 1987, Antony Gormley, Collection of the Modern Art Museum of Fort Worth. Gift of Anne Burnett Tandy in Memory of Ollie Lake Burnett, by Exchange.

# Putting It All Together

The final chapter includes three sections: *One-Two-Three, Museum Adventure,* and *Make a Museum*. Each provides examples for utilizing these warm-up and interpretive activities in accessible and adaptable ways. Both traditional and alternative ideas for instruction are included to inspire use in the classroom, museum, and virtual environments. *One-Two-Three* recommends engaging combinations of warm-up and interpretive activities. Additionally, suggestions for connecting learning objectives with teaching strategies offer educators solutions for linking art and learners. These suggestions can be used directly or adapted to suit individual curriculums.

The second section, *Museum Adventure,* provides educators a practical guide to facilitate a successful museum experience. Finally, *Make a Museum,* includes ideas to create virtual museums, to extend existing museum experiences, and to provide alternatives if a museum visit is not possible.

Now all we need is to put it all together!

## One-Two-Three

The following is a list of suggested combinations of warm-up and interpretive activities with possible connections to existing curricula. These suggestions can be used to suit individual needs and unit designs:

**One**    *Be the Element* or *Form a Shape*
**Two**    *Elementary, My Dear Artist*
**Three**   Adapt to existing activities featuring abstract and nonobjective works of art and production activities.

**One**    *Gesture Guess*
**Two**    *You're Invited!*
**Three**   Adapt to activities featuring portraits or self-portraits.

**One**    *Making Metaphors*
**Two**    *Art Diary*
**Three**   Adapt to activities that feature a focus of expressive art.

**One**    *1-800-ART-TALK*
**Two**    *Be A Curator*
**Three**   Adapt to activities featuring creating art around a theme.

**One**    *Be A Curator*
**Two**    *Be A Museum Educator*
**Three**   Adapt to activities encompassing careers in art.

**One**    *Apples to Apples*
**Two**    *Learning Through Lenses*
**Three**   Adapt to activities featuring multicultural art such as Mexican Muralists.

**One**    *Back Track*
**Two**    *Step-by-step*
**Three**   Adapt to activities featuring origami.

**One**    *Form a Shape*
**Two**    *Sculpt-Your Clay*
**Three**   Adapt to activities featuring ceramics.

**One**    *Play Three*
**Two**    *Meaning-TV*
**Three**   Adapt to activities featuring performance art.

**One**    *Point of View* and/or *Morph Art*
**Two**    *Subject Sleuth*
**Three**   Adapt to activities featuring architecture.

**One**    *Personality Profile*
**Two**    *You're Invited!*
**Three**   Adapt to activities featuring artists' self-portraits.

| | |
|---|---|
| **One** | *Sound Symphony* |
| **Two** | *Compare and Contrast* |
| **Three** | Adapt to activities featuring landscape. |

| | |
|---|---|
| **One** | *Totally Texture* |
| **Two** | *Back in Time* |
| **Three** | Adapt to activities featuring *trompe l'oeil* techniques. |

| | |
|---|---|
| **One** | *Puzzling* |
| **Two** | *Discover Art* |
| **Three** | Adapt to activities featuring M.C. Escher and tesselations. |

| | |
|---|---|
| **One** | *Word Search* then *Cinquain Poem* |
| **Two** | *Discover Art* |
| **Three** | Adapt to activities featuring the works of one artist. |

| | |
|---|---|
| **One** | *Be the Element* |
| **Two** | *Step-by-step* |
| **Three** | Adapt to activities featuring color theory. |

| | |
|---|---|
| **One** | *Matching Metaphors* |
| **Two** | *Dear . . .* |
| **Three** | Adapt to bookmaking to create an *Art Diary*. |

| | |
|---|---|
| **One** | *A Friend for Life* |
| **Two** | *Experience Art* |
| **Three** | Adapt to activities featuring the creation of a work of art based on the writings. |

| | |
|---|---|
| **One** | *If Art Could Talk* |
| **Two** | *Back in Time* |
| **Three** | Adapt to activities involved with creating interdisciplinary timelines. |

| | |
|---|---|
| **One** | *I Packed my Bag* |
| **Two** | *Travel Brochure* |
| **Three** | Adapt to activities featuring *plein air* landscape painting or fantasy landscapes or a graphic design unit. |

| | |
|---|---|
| **One** | *Fan Poem* |
| **Two** | *Quality Quotes* |
| **Three** | Adapt to language activities extending *Art For Sale*. |

These suggestions can be used to suit individual needs and curricula. *Museum Adventure* offers parents and educators a guide for facilitating a successful museum experience. *Make a Museum* provides inspiration for creating virtual museums, for extending existing museum experiences, or for providing alternatives if a museum visit is not possible.

## Museum Adventure

*Museum Adventure* offers suggestions for facilitating a successful museum experience.

### Museum Etiquette
Visiting a museum should be a fun, enjoyable experience for all. One of the ways to ensure a positive adventure is to exercise appropriate museum etiquette. The following is practical advice for both the novice and experienced museum visitor.

The desire to touch works of art is one of the most challenging obstacles of a museum visit. The *Mirror* activity is a great warm-up before entering a museum or beginning a tour.

### Mirror
- Begin with a clean mirror.
- Have participants form a circle.
- Have each participant press a finger on the mirror and pass it around the circle.
- Discuss the surface of the mirror with fingerprints and without fingerprints.
- Draw a comparison between fingerprints on the mirror and fingerprints on a work of art.
- What would happen if every visitor in a museum touches a work of art?

### Remind participants that . . .
- it is okay to talk about art.
- food and drink are saved for lunch.
- all parts of the body should remain at least two feet away from works of art and others; just like you, works of art have a comfort zone.
- it is okay to touch with your eyes, but not with your hands (this includes walls, labels, and display cabinets).
- pens, pencils, or sharp objects should not be used for pointing; some museums do not allow them in the galleries.
- walk (do not run) through the galleries so you do not miss your favorite work of art of the day.
- have a signal to obtain immediate control of your group. Instruct the participants to *Freeze* at a given signal. Everyone must stop and *Freeze!* This command may prevent bumps or accidents from occurring in the museum.
- Encourage them to have fun!

### Museum Experiences
A little planning goes a long way to ensure a successful museum experience:

- Large groups (10+): call the museum educator or tour coordinator at least four weeks in advance. Discuss possibilities for relating your visit with the existing curriculum. Be flexible.
- Smaller groups (1-9): call the museum educator or tour coordinator regarding public tour schedules or special activities.
- Inform the museum educator or tour coordinator the age group you will be bringing and any special needs of participants.
- Bring a sweater or light jacket as temperatures can be uncomfortably cool to conserve the art.
- Make sure you have a map of how to get to the museum.
- Know what is on exhibition to prevent surprise.

### *Pack your bag with . . .*
▲ tissue.
▲ a small pencil-sharpener in a plastic bag.
▲ name tags with participants' first name.
▲ a list of phone numbers: transportation coordinator, school, and museum; name of the docent or tour guide.
▲ snacks for breaks outside the galleries.
▲ a list of all participants.

### *At the museum:*
▲ Pick up a floor plan of the museum.
▲ Locate restrooms and water fountains.
▲ Sit and relax if tired.
▲ Souvenirs provide excellent memory of the adventure.
▲ Have fun!

## Make A Museum

*Make a Museum* provides inspiration for creating virtual museums, for extending existing museum experiences, or for providing alternatives if a museum visit is not possible.

- Create a **gallery** at home on a rainy day and give tours for neighbors.

- Create a student-developed gallery with **docents**, **curators**, director, graphic designers, and student-written labels.

- Create a virtual gallery utilizing available technology resources.

- **Exhibit** student work at local businesses.

- Create on-line portfolios for an electronic gallery.

- Display works of community artists in local schools (running exhibition).

- Rotate an exhibition of framed student work in school.

- Create a rotating family gallery in one room in the house.

- Create a reproduction gallery in schools and homes.

- Collect postcards from museum visits to create timelines and mini-galleries and for sorting activities.

- Have student art reporters interview student artists, local artists, gallery owners, and museums for art in the student newspapers, local newspapers, and magazine articles.

- Arrange with a gallery owner for exhibitions.

- Organize tours to local art museums.

- Create collaborative exhibitions between schools and communities.

- Visit artists and their studios.

- Make a studio in the house.

# Resources

The handbook would be incomplete without resources to assist educators in experiencing art. Activity worksheets and cards are ready to be copied and used by learners. The glossary section provides accessible definitions of uncommon terms and jargon; glossary words are in **bold type**. Finally, for additional information on art and art museum education techniques, a list of materials used for *Experience Art* and a list of related readings are included in the Selected Readings sections.

**Bodily-Kinesthetic Cards**

| | |
|---|---|
| Look for a work of art that moves you. What is it about the work of art that causes you to feel this way? | Look for a work of art that moves you. What does it tell you about your own life? |
| Look for a work of art that seems to call to you. Ask the work, "What do you have to tell me about my life?" Wait until you have a response. | Look for a work of art that reminds you about something from your past. What is it about this piece that reminds you of the past? |
| Look for a work of art that speaks to you emotionally. Take time to look and think about it thoroughly. Notice changing sensations, thoughts, or memories. | Look for a work of art that speaks to you emotionally. Take time to look and think about it thoroughly. Describe your feelings. |
| Choose a gallery and a work of art that you think is very likely to evoke a similar emotional response when anyone sees it. What are the reasons for your choice? | Look for a work of art that gives you clues about the artist's personality, feelings, or values. How does the work communicate these clues? |
| Find a work of art that is like you. What are the similarities? | |

Adapted from Ray Williams, Ackland Art Museum

Resources | Worksheets

## Personality Profile Worksheet

Place the image of the work of art here.

Name: _____

Date of birth: _____

Birthplace: _____

Favorite color: _____

My last meal was: _____

Last book read: _____

Favorite car: _____

Favorite quote: _____

I believe in: _____

My hero is: _____

My favorite artist is: _____

Behind my back people say I am: _____

People like me because: _____

Most valued possession: _____

**Cinquain Poem Worksheet**                                    **Linguistic**

———————————————
Line 1
NOUN
(Person, Place, or Thing)

———————————  ———————————
Line 2
TWO ADJECTIVES
(Describe the noun)

—————————  —————————  —————————
Line 3
THREE VERBS
(Action or "ing" words)

————————  ————————  ————————  ————————
Line 4
FOUR WORD PHRASE
(Describe the noun)

———————————————
Line 5
NOUN
(Person, Place, or Thing)

## Dear . . . Worksheet                                                              Linguistic

Date _____

Dear _____,

_____

_____

_____

_____

_____

_____

_____

_____

_____

_____

_____

_____

_____

_____

_____

                                        _____,

                                        _____

## Dear . . . Postcard Worksheet **Linguistic**

**Front of Postcard**

Date_____

Dear_____,

_____

_____

_____

_____

_____

_____

_____

_____

*Experience Art: A Handbook for Teaching and Learning with Works of Art Postcard*

From:

_____

_____

_____

To:

_____

_____

_____

_____

Place
Stamp
Here

**Back of Postcard**

## The Real Thing, Baby! Worksheet                    **Logical-Mathematical**

Is your image as BIG as a car?

_____

Or as small as a stamp?

_____

Which way is up?

_____

What do you think the title is?

_____

What are the materials?

_____

How many colors are there? Name them:

_____

_____

What would it feel like if you could touch it?

_____

_____

How is the surface different on the reproduction than on the real thing?

_____

_____

Name five ways the real thing is different than the work of art. Similar?

_____

_____

_____

_____

_____

Is it important to experience the real thing? Why or why not?

_____

_____

| **Art Diary Worksheet** | **Content Discovered** |

## Descriptive Words

Straight Lines            Stiff
Curved Lines              Soft
Rectangles                Vase Shapes
Numbers                   Parts of Animals
Simple                    Plant Shapes
Ornate                    Shell Shapes
Patterns                  3-D Carving
Formal                    Plain
Casual                    Geometric Shapes
Heavy                     Decorative Names
Textural                  Closed-In-Form
Colorful                  Light
Worn                      Painterly

## Questions

1. Who made the work of art?

_____

2. When?

_____

3. Where?

_____

4. Of what materials?

_____

_____

5. What was its main purpose?

_____

_____

6. What additional purposes may it have served?

_____

_____

7. What other objects does this object most closely resemble?

_____

_____

## **Elementary, My Dear Artist** Worksheet          **Content Discovered**

Using the assigned element:

1. Locate the work of art within which the element is found.

   Title: _____

   Artist: _____

2. Consider how your interpretation (impression) of the work might be different if . . .

   The element was bigger:

   _____
   _____
   _____

   The element was smaller:

   _____
   _____
   _____

   The element changed to a different color:

   _____
   _____
   _____

   If you could change the color, what would you change it to?

   _____

   The element was placed somewhere else in the work:

   _____
   _____

   The element was turned upside down or sideways:

   _____
   _____

   The element changed shape:

   _____
   _____

   The element multiplied:

   _____

   The element was taken away from the work entirely:

   _____

| Learning Through Lenses Lens Cards | Content Discovered |
|---|---|

### Formal Analysis

Describe the elements of art and principles of design within this work of art.

### Multicultural Analysis

What cultures or backgrounds do you think influence the art? The artist? Which influence your interpretation? Consider each individual's background and culture.

### Multisensory Analysis

Investigate senses other than visual captured or expressed in the work of art. Reenact the scene, event, or expression the work of art describes.

### Feminist Analysis

Consider the influence of gender on both the creation and interpretation of the work of art. Would this work have a different message if made by someone from the opposite sex?

### Reconstructionist Analysis

Consider the mental and physical processes of the artist and materials utilized on the work of art. Would the meaning be different if this work of art was created in a different media?

**Venn Diagram** Worksheet                    **Content Discovered**

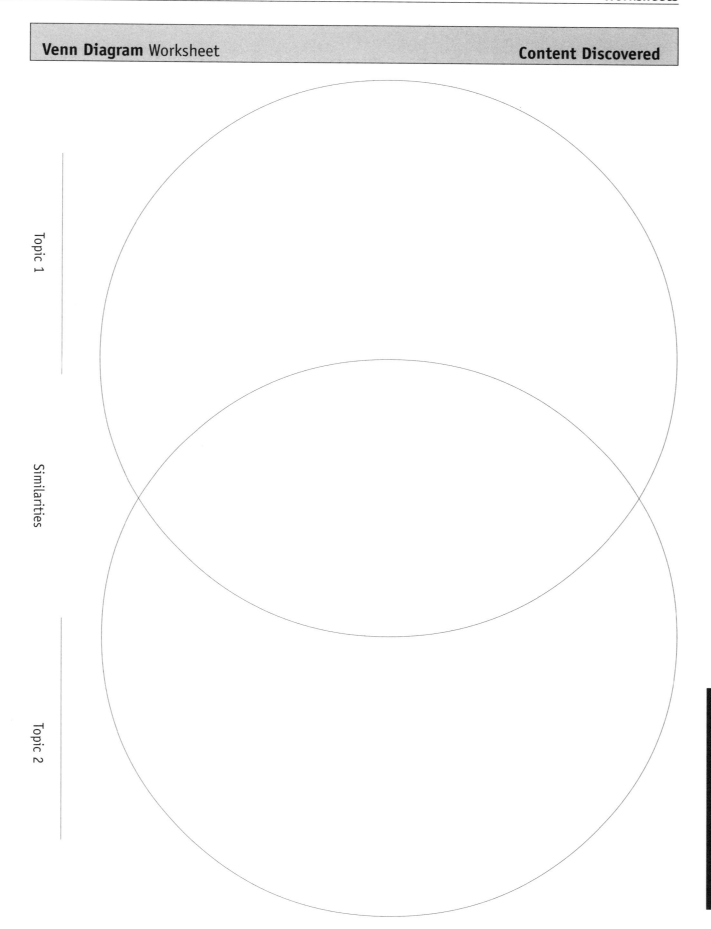

Topic 1

Similarities

Topic 2

## Create a Tour Worksheet                    Content Given

*Develop a tour with art which . . .*

tells a story

was originally part of architecture or buildings

is about feelings

was intended for a useful purpose (function)

has a religious or spiritual purpose

expresses the artists's imagination

shows a lot of skill

shows how the artist was experimenting with materials

is very delicate and refined

is somewhat rough or "unfinished"

is surprising

is very old

is from your city, or is about things, people, places recognizable

is very difficult to tell what the artist had in mind

uses similar media

is created by members of a similar culture

has similar symbols

has a social message

Adapted from Ray Williams, Ackland Art Museum

**Quoting Art** Worksheet                              **Content Given**

"Art is not practical, and shouldn't be practical. Painting and sculpting . . . are there to make life more interesting, more wonderful than it would be without them."

**—Henry Moore**

"The first requirement, fundamental to all others, is that the subject matter and the narrative (of a painting) be grandiose, such as battles, heroic action, and religious themes."

**—Nicolas Poussin**

"The artwork is not the paint on the canvas or the print on the page; it is the moment of creation by the artist and the moment of understanding by the viewer."

**—Walker Percy**

"A rapid rendering of a landscape represents only one moment of its appearance. I . . . prefer to discover its more enduring character and content, even at the risk of sacrificing some of its more pleasant qualities."

**—Henri Matisse**

"The artist is a cool Spectator-Reporter in the Arena of Hot Events."

**—Stuart Davis**

"The job of the artist is to always deepen the mystery."

**—Francis Bacon**

"The function of the creative artist consists of making laws, not in following laws already made."

**—Ferruccio Busoni**

"Art evokes the mystery without which the word would not exist."

**—René-Francois-Magritte**

"Art is a technique of communication. The image is the most complete technique of all communication."

**—Claes Oldenburg**

"Painting is just another way of keeping a diary."

**—Pablo Picasso**

"No amount of skillful invention can replace the essential element of imagination."

**—Edward Hopper**

**Resources**

**Worksheets**

**What Does it Mean to You?** Worksheet            **Content Given**

## Viewing Strategies

Select five viewing strategies. Rank them 1-5 with one being the best strategy.

_____   Make a diagram to show how the artist organized the main shapes.

_____   Ask a question about the time in history when the work was made.

_____   Look for clues about how the artwork was made.

_____   List all the objects you see.

_____   Tell what the work reminds you of.

_____   Relate the art to something in your own life.

_____   Compare the work you choose to another one in the same room.

_____   Describe your first reaction.

_____   Tell what made you choose this work of art.

_____   Make the same pose and facial expression you see in the figure.

_____   Ask for more information about the artist.

_____   Write down your biggest question and ask the leader.

_____   Go to the library and find out more about the country it is from.

_____   Imagine a story that fits what you see.

_____   Write down a conversation between two people in the artwork.

_____   Find the focal point.

_____   Make the sounds you could hear in this picture.

_____   Talk about it with a friend.

Adapted from Ray Williams, Ackland Art Museum

# Glossary

**abstract**: a term referring to the visual effects that derive their appearance from natural objects but which have been simplified and/or rearranged to satisfy artists' needs for organization or expression.

**A.C.E.**: After Common Era, a less Western-centered term than A.D. (Anno Domini, in the year of Our Lord).

**aesthetics**: philosophical considerations and questions about the nature of art in general; three key questions are: what is art? what is beautiful? and is it art?

**aesthetician**: one who studies aesthetics.

**art critic**: a person who shares thoughtful judgments about art.

**art historian**: a person that acquires knowledge about the contributions artists and art make to culture and society.

**artifact**: an object created by a human being.

**artist**: an individual who professes and practices one of the fine arts.

**Barnes, Albert C.**: a notoriously candid self-made millionaire who became an avid art collector to educate the masses with his philosophy about art.

**B.C.E.**: Before Common Era, the replacement for B.C. (before Christ).

**cinquain**: a style of poetry that follows a format of:
  Line 1: noun
  Line 2: 2 adjectives
  Line 3: 3 verbs
  Line 4: 4-word phrase
  Line 5: noun

**composition**: ordered arrangement of elements in a work of art, usually according to the principles of design.

**Contemporary Art**: art of the last half of the 20th century.

**content**: the information and subject matter of a work, refers to the significance, meaning, and value of a work of art.

**context:** the meaning surrounding a work of art which cannot be entirely understood or revealed if the work is experienced in isolation; the work must be seen and interpreted in relation (or context) to the culture in which it was produced, the prominent ideas in the history of art when the work was made.

**critical thinking:** thinking on a high level. Goes beyond listing what one can see in a work of art; to question, predict, or interpret works of art through its visual clues.

**criticism:** responding to, interpreting meaning, and making critical judgments about specific works of art or styles.

**critique:** responding to and making judgments about the properties and qualities that exist in a work of art.

**culture:** a society or civilization marked by distinctive concepts, habits, skills, implementations, and art forms.

**curate:** the act of organizing works of art for an exhibition.

**curator:** a person who gathers information about each work of art in an exhibition and decides how to display it.

**docent:** a guide, facilitator and/or teacher for visitors to a museum; from Latin, docere, meaning to teach.

**elements of art:** the graphic devices with which the artist works, such as line, color, texture, value, space and shape.

**exhibit:** to show or display works of art.

**exhibition:** an organized show of works of art.

**figure:** a person represented in a work of art.

**gallery:** a specific section of a museum (ex. The Gallery of the Americas), or a place of business where art is displayed or sold.

**gallery etiquette:** the expected behaviors appropriate for visitors to the art museum or gallery. See the *Putting it Together* section.

**Gardner, Howard:** a cognitive psychologist best known for his research and rationale of multiple intelligences and its affiliated educational laboratory, Harvard's Project Zero.

**geometric:** shapes or forms that can be defined by mathematical formulas. Basic geometric shapes are the square, circle, triangle. Basic geometric forms are the cube, sphere, and pyramid.

**Getty, J. Paul:** an eccentric multi-billionaire responsible for creating the Getty Museum of Art in Malibu, California, and whose fortune forms the basis for the J. Paul Getty Trust.

**Greenberg, Clement:** famous art critic, most well-known for an approach to criticism of modern art called formalism.

**Haiku:** a Japanese form of poetry that follows this format:
        Line 1: 5 syllable phrase
        Line 2: 7 syllable phrase
        Line 3: 5 syllable phrase

**Hughes, Robert:** art critic and author of American Visions.

**illustration:** images that are usually associated with commercial purposes, often intended to accompany and complement written text.

**interactive:** the learner is an active participant in the educational experience.

**interpretation:** an attempt to arrive at an understanding of the meaning of a work of art.

**landscape:** a work of art in which the compositional elements include land forms; a depiction of nature.

**mind mapping:** mind mapping was developed in the late 1960s by Tony Buzan as a non-linear visualization of a concept or idea which can be easily linked and cross-referenced as the creator makes connections. In fact, hypertext markup language (HTML) and the World Wide Web's (WWW) linking and jumping capabilities were designed with similar goals. Students are empowered to make note-taking and idea-generating more accessible to memory by more closely mimicking the human brain's functions.

**mobile:** a suspended sculpture with parts that can be moved, especially by air currents.

**multiple interpretations:** the existence of pluralistic points of view, a form of the new art histories' postmodernist acceptance of different perspectives of the derivation of a meaning.

**museum:** an institution which collects, preserves, researches, displays, and educates from a collection of objects for the general public viewing and response.

**museum etiquette:** the expected behaviors appropriate for visitors to the art museum or gallery. See the Putting it Together section.

**nonobjective:** works of art without discernible subject matter.

**opaque:** the opposite of transparent; unable to be seen through.

**organic:** irregular and uneven shapes or forms. Their outlines are curved, uneven, angular, or all three. These shapes and forms are often found in nature.

**personify:** giving inanimate objects human qualities and behaviors.

**Postmodern:** beginning in the mid-1980's, this era is characterized by the exploration and acceptance of multiple viewpoints in a nonhierarchical, nonlinear, multicultural manner.

**principles of design:** guides for planning relationships among visual elements in works of art; balance, rhythm, proportion, pattern, unity, and variety.

Resources

Glossary

**print:** the result of an artistic process of pulling an image off a plate or block. Several printing techniques include intaglio, relief, and lithography.

**process:** the sequence of steps an artist must undergo when creating a work of art.

**representational art:** works of art which contain recognizable subject matter, not necessarily realistic.

**reproduction:** a copy of a work of art. Posters and postcards are examples of reproductions.

**rhythm:** a principle of design that indicates a type of movement in an work of art, often by repeated shapes, lines, or colors.

**seascape:** a work of art in which compositional elements include images of the sea.

**sign:** that which represents an idea or conveys meaning beyond the literal, more personal and individual than a symbol.

**still life:** a group of inanimate objects arranged to be painted or drawn; also a painting or drawing of stationary objects.

**style:** the distinctive characteristics contained in the works of art of a person, period of time, or geographic location.

**subject:** topic, a person, animal, etc. a matter under consideration or discussion.

**symbol:** that which represents an idea or conveys meaning beyond the literal, more universal than a sign, such as religious icons.

**tactile:** the physical activity of touching.

**theme:** over-arching idea or concept such as environmental concerns or belief systems.

**three-dimensional:** artwork which has height, width, and depth (volume). It is not flat.

**two-dimensional:** artwork which has height and width. It is flat.

**Venn Diagram:** a visual diagram consisting of two overlapping circles used to compare and contrast two items. The inside of each circle represents each item being studied and the overlapping area represents the commonalities of the items.

**Virtual Exhibitions:** an exhibition where the works of art are usually created, digitized, or scanned into a computer to be viewed.

**visual:** relating to sight; what you can see.

**web:** similar to mind mapping, although webs do not necessarily include interconnecting branches and links.

# Selected Readings

**Books, Presentations, and Papers**

Alexander, E. P. (1979). *Museums in motion: An introduction to the history and functions of museums*. Nashville: American Association for State and Local History.

American Association of Museums. (1992). *Excellence and equity: education and the public dimension of museums*. Washington, D.C.: American Association of Museums.

American Association of Museums. (1994, Winter). Board diversity: change begins at the top in *Excellence and equity*. Washington, D.C.: American Association of Museums.

Barrett, T. (1994). *Criticizing art: Understanding the contemporary*. Mountain View, CA: Mayfield Publishing Company.

Brommer, G. (1997). *Discovering Art History*. Worcester, MA: Davis Publications, Inc.

Brommer, G. & Kinne, N. (1995) *Exploring Painting, second edition*. Worcester, MA: Davis Publications, Inc.

Broudy, H. (1987). *The role of imagery in learning*. Los Angeles, CA: The Getty Education Institute for the Arts.

Buzan, T. & Buzan, B. (1993). *The mind map book*. New York: The Penguin Group.

Commission of Museums for a New Century. (1984). *Museums for a new century*. Washington, D.C.: American Association of Museums.

Corrin, L. & Wilson, F. (1992). Mining the museum 1& 2. *Discipline-based art education and cultural diversity*. Seminar Proceedings Sixth Plenary Session: Affinity Group Summary Reports. Los Angeles: Getty Publications.

Cullen, J. (1992) In defense of overinterpretation in Collini, S. (Ed.) *Umberto Eco: Interpretation and overinterpretation*. Cambridge: Cambridge University Press.

de Varine-Bohan, H. (1976) The modern museum: Requirements and problems of a new approach, in Hooper-Greenhill, E. (Ed) *The educational role of the museum*. London and New York:  Routledge.

Dierking, L. D. (1989). The family museum experience: Implications from research, in *Patterns in Practice*. Washington D.C.: Museum Education Roundtable.

Dobbs, S. M. (1992). *The DBAE handbook: An overview of discipline-based art education*. Santa Monica, CA: The Getty Education Institute for the Arts.

Eisner, E. (1987*). The role of discipline-based art education in America's schools*. Santa Monica, California: The Getty Education Institute for the Arts.

Erickson, M. & Katter, E. (1991). *Token Response*. Tucson, Arizona: Crizmac Art and Cultural Education Materials.

Evans, G. (1995). Learning and the physical environment, in *Public Institutions for Personal Learning*. Washington D.C.: American Association of Museums.

Falk, J. H., Ph.D., & Dierking, L. D., Ph.D. (1992). *The museum experience*. Washington, D.C.: Whalesback Books.

Falk, J. H., Ph.D., & Dierking, L. D., Ph.D. (Eds). (1995). *Public institutions for personal learning: Establishing a research agenda*. Washington, D.C.: American Association of Museums.

Frankel, D. (1995). *Masterpieces: The best-loved paintings from America's museums*. New York, New York: Simon & Schuster.

Gardner, H. (1990). *Art education and human development*. Los Angeles, CA: The Getty Education Institute for the Arts.

Hamblen, K. (1993) The emergence of Neo-DBAE. Paper presented at the Annual Meeting of the American Educational research Association (Atlanta, GA, April 12-16, 1993).

Hirzy, E. C. (1995, Winter). Shared vision or dueling agendas? in *Excellence and equity*. Washington D.C.: American Association of Museums.

Hooper-Greenhill, E. (1994). *The educational role of the museum*. London: Routledge.

Hodge, R. & D'Souza W. (1994) The museum as a communicator: a semiotic analysis of the Western Australian Gallery, Perth, in Hooper Greenhill, E. (Ed), *The educational role of the museum*. London and New York: Routledge.

Housen, A. with Miller, N. L. and Yenawine, P. (1991). MoMA research and evaluation study: School programs. The Museum of Modern Art, New York.

*Insights: museums, visitors, attitudes, and expectations: A focus group experiment* (1991). Los Angeles: The Getty Education Institute for the Arts.

Jensen, N. and Munley, M. E. (1989). Training for museum education professionals, in *Patterns in Practice*. Washington D.C.: Museum Education Roundtable.

Mayer, M. (1996) *Precious minds and precious objects: Implications of the new art histories for art museum education*. Unpublished dissertation proposal, Pennsylvania State University.

McCarter, R. W., Ed. D., & Walkup, N. (Eds.). (1996). *North Texas institute for the visual arts: Participant handbook*. Denton, Texas: University of North Texas.

Museum Education Committee (1990). *Statement on professional standards for museum education*. Washington D.C.: American Association of Museums.

Newsom, B. & Silver, A. (Eds.) (1978) *The art museum as educator*. Berkeley, LA, London: The University of California Press.

Nicholson, C. (1996, Spring). Just a little respect, in *The Docent Educator*. Seattle, Washington: Minds in Motion.

Ott, R. (1989). Teaching criticism in museums, in Berry, N. & Mayer, S. (Eds.) *Museum education*: History, theory and practice. Reston, VA: National Art Education Association.

Parks, M. E. (1994). *The art teacher's desktop reference*. New Jersey: Prentice Hall.

Patterson, W. (1989). Object contemplation: Theory into practice, in *Patterns in practice*. Washington D.C.: Museum Education Roundtable.

Perkins, D. (1994). *The intelligent eye: Learning to think by looking at art*. Santa Monica, CA: The Getty Center for Education in the Arts.

Smith, R. (1989). *Discipline-based art education: Origins, meaning, and development*. Reston, VA: National Art Education Association.

Sternberg, S. (1989) The art of participation, in Berry & Mayer (Eds.) Museum education: History, theory, and practice. Reston, VA: National Art Education Association, p. 154-171.

The Arts in General Education Project of the University City, Missouri, Schools & The Aesthetic Education Program of CEMREL, Inc. (1971). *Theatre game file*. St. Louis, Missouri: CEMREL, Inc.

Yenawine, P. (1988) Master teaching in an art museum, in *Patterns and practice*: Selections from the Journal of Museum Education. Washington, D.C.: Museum Education Roundtable.

Yenawine, P. (1989/90) Preliminary Report - Year I (1989/90), MoMA Research and Evaluation Study: School Programs

Zeller, T. The history and philosophical foundations of art museum education in America, in Berry, N. & Mayer, S. (Eds.) Museum education: History, theory and practice. Reston, VA: National Art Education Association.

Resources

Selected Readings

**Electronic Document**

Duke, L. (1996c). Visual thinking strategies: A learner-centered approach to using art in education online.
http://www.art.uiuc.edu/kam/vts/premise.html

**Journals**

Adams, M. (1995, Fall). Museum professionals in conversation. *Journal of Museum Education.*

Bal, M. & Bryson, N. (1991, June) Semiotics and art history. *Art Bulletin* 123 (2), p. 188-191.

Brown, C. K. (1995, Fall) A national conversation: Speaking of and from museums. *Journal of Museum Education.*

Chryslee, G. J. (1995, Winter). Creating museums that change people's lives: Operationalizing the notion of restorative environments. *Journal of Museum Education.*

Csikszentmihalyi, M. and Hermanson, K. (1995, May/June). Intrinsic motivation in museums: What makes visitors want to learn? in *Museum News.* Washington D.C.: American Association of Museums.

Davis, J., Gardner, H. (1993) Open windows, open doors, in *Museum News.* 72(1).

Dunn, P. (1996). More power: Integrated interactive technology and art education, in *Art Education.* 49(6), 6-11.

Durant, S-R. (1996, January). Reflections on museum education at Dulwich Picture Gallery, in *Art Education.*

Edson, G. (1995, Winter). The quanderies of museum training, in *Journal of Museum Education.*

Faunce, S. (1992, Jan/Feb). Theory and practice, in *Museum News*, Vol. 71, No.1.

Funch, B. S. (1993) Educating the eye: Strategies for museum education, in *Journal of Aesthetics Education*, Vol 27, No. 1, Spring.

Galbraith, L. (1993, September) Familiar, interactive and collaborative pedagogy: Changing practices in preservice art education, in *Art Education* 46(5), p. 6-11.

Gurian, E. H. (1995, Fall) Offering safer public spaces, in *Journal of Museum Education.*

Hackney, S. (Fall, 1995). NEH's national conversation: A quest for common ground, in *Journal of Museum Education.*

Hirsch, J. S. and Landau, J. A. (1995, Fall) The national conversation: pluralism and diversity in museum offerings, in *Journal of Museum Education.*

Hord, S. M. (1986, February). A synthesis of research on organizational collaboration, in *Educational Leadership*.

Julian, J. (1997, May) In a postmodern backpack: Basics for the art teacher on-line, in *Art Education*. 50(23) p. 23-24, 41-42.

Kaplan, S. with Bardwell, L. V. and Slakter, D. B. (1993, Fall). The restorative experience as a museum benefit, in *Journal of Museum Education*, Vol. 18 No. 3.

Keifer-Boyd, K. (1996) Interfacing hypermedia and the internet with critical inquiry in the arts: Preservice training, in *Art Education*. 49(6), 33-41.

Walsh-Piper, K. (1994, Fall). Museum education and the aesthetic experience, in *Journal of Aesthetic Education*.